Evergreens

KENNETH A. BECKETT

Cassell

The Royal Horticultural Society

THE ROYAL HORTICULTURAL SOCIETY

Cassell Educational Limited
Villiers House, 41/47 Strand
London WC2N 5JE
for the Royal Horticultural Society

First published 1990

British Library Cataloguing in Publication Data
Beckett, Kenneth A. (Kenneth Albert)
  Evergreens.
  1. Gardens. Evergreen plants
  I. Title   II. Royal Horticultural Society   III. Series
  635

  ISBN 0-304-31852-3

Photographs by Gillian Beckett

Phototypesetting by Chapterhouse Ltd, Formby
Printed in Hong Kong by Wing King Tong Co. Ltd

Cover: Photinia × fraseri 'Red Robin', with its bright young
foliage, creates from a distance the illusion of a shrub in
full bloom
Frontispiece: Evergreen shrubs display a range of habits,
colours and leaf shapes
Back cover: The lovely Berberis valdiviana is uncommon,
but well worth seeking out

Contents

Introduction

Surprisingly enough, the word 'evergreens' can still conjure up in some gardeners' minds the image of an overgrown Victorian shrubbery, often under trees, composed of gaunt and dusty specimens of evergreen spindle, spotted laurel and privet. Happily, the reality of that image is fast disappearing as more people appreciate the value and aesthetic appeal of evergreens.

Wherever they are planted in the garden, evergreens add a richness of texture and hue that most deciduous plants cannot emulate. This is because the durability of evergreen leaves demands that they should be thicker and stronger. In many species, this thickness concentrates the green pigments or chlorophyll and gives the leaves a deep or richer colour. It might be thought that such depth of hue would create a sombre effect, but this is seldom so. To withstand winter gales, evergreen foliage often has a waxy or polished surface and this adds that quality of lustre which is so much a feature of the species most highly valued horticulturally.

Shades of green are not all that the leaves of evergreens offer us. A large number have young foliage which is bronze, coppery or red-flushed. A good example of the latter is *Photinia × fraseri* and its cultivars, in particular 'Red Robin', which has young leaves as bright as a flower. Other evergreens are grey or grey-green – for example, some of the sun roses and hebes. Sometimes, as in *Elaeagnus macrophylla*, the leaves are silvery beneath and green above, catching the light when turned in the wind.

Foliage size, shape, density and stance also play a key role in deciding how any plant presents its green-ness to the light and to the eye of the beholder. Such factors alone can dictate whether a plant charms us or not and this is particularly true of evergreens. Indeed, on the whole evergreens score heavily against their deciduous counterparts under these criteria. Take leaf shape. Among reasonably hardy plants, what deciduous tree can provide such architectural magnificence as the bull bay, *Magnolia grandiflora*? And what deciduous shrub can rival *Fatsia japonica*?

The density and stance of leaves go hand-in-hand in matters of

The magnificent leaves and flowers of *Magnolia grandiflora* make it a highly desirable evergreen

overall appeal. Evergreen shrubs with crowded small leaves give us a richness of texture rarely, if ever, equalled by deciduous shrubs. The various kinds of box, the much maligned *Lonicera nitida*, and the less than hardy *Pittosporum tenuifolium* are all excellent when it comes to providing restful background greenery. Leaf stance can do much for the character of a plant. Consider, for instance, the almost fiercely erect blades of *Prunus laurocerasus* 'Otto Luyken' and the positively pendulous leaves of *Eucalyptus*.

For a specimen plant, overall outline is important and here again evergreens have the edge over deciduous trees and shrubs. One only has to think of the impressive columns, spires and pyramids of conifers or the billowing roundness of the holm oak, *Quercus ilex*.

As if foliage were not enough, some evergreens produce a show of flowers to compete with or surpass the best that deciduous subjects can provide. In some cases, such as *Mahonia aquifolium*, a profligate number of small flowers creates the display. At the other end of the scale are the immense and spectacular wide-open goblets of *Magnolia grandiflora*. In addition, many evergreens have colourful fruits as an autumn and winter attraction.

For all these reasons, it makes sense to use evergreen trees and shrubs in the garden. Over and above their basic merits is the splendid bonus of winter cheer. Winter is, after all, *the* season when green and living things can brighten even dismal wet days. Evergreens, both in drifts and as specimens, will blend or contrast with their deciduous companions for much of the year, but when the last leaf falls in autumn, they come into full prominence and keep the garden scene satisfying and interesting until spring.

As used in this book, the word evergreens refers to trees and shrubs which stay green in winter. However, camellias, rhododendrons, heaths and heathers, ivies and most conifers have not been included because there are already separate Wisley Handbooks devoted to their use and culture (see inside back cover). Other Wisley Handbooks relevant to evergreens or dealing with particular aspects that are not treated in detail here are *Alpines the Easy Way, Climbing and Wall Plants, Ground Cover Plants, Seaside Gardening, Shrubs for Small Gardens, Trees for Small Gardens* and *The Winter Garden*.

Mahonia 'Undulata' gives a spectacular effect with a mass of small flowers

Where to Grow Evergreens

IN MIXED BORDERS AND BEDS

As most of the attractive hardy evergreens are shrubs, it is sensible to use them as an integral part of a shrub or mixed border. Selected with some imagination, they will not only provide interest in their own right with foliage and possibly flowers or fruits, but supply winter greenery and act as a foil for late autumn- to early spring-blooming deciduous shrubs. For instance, the taller evergreen shrubs can be planted as the centrepiece of a bed, or the backbone of a border, ideally with drifts of smaller ones near the front, and the middle distance can then be filled with choice flowering deciduous shrubs. By first getting familiar with both the deciduous and evergreen shrubs you would like to plant, it is possible to make associations both harmonious and contrasting. An obvious example of the latter is to use one of the large-leaved hollies, say *Ilex* × *altaclerensis* 'Hodginsii', as a backdrop for the rich yellow winter flowers of *Hamamelis mollis*. If you have a shady spot, try a mixed planting of the evergreen *Skimmia japonica* with the deciduous *Daphne mezereum*.

The smaller evergreen shrubs can play a subservient role as high ground cover in a mainly or totally deciduous shrub bed or border. Useful are *Berberis*, *Sarcococca* and *Cotoneaster*, but make sure that you put sun-lovers in front and shade-tolerant ones further in.

AS FOCAL POINTS

One of the most pleasing garden practices is the use of especially attractive plants as focal points or specimens – for example, a tree at the head of a vista, or a shrub at the junction of a path or in a lawn. What better than to choose an evergreen for such a position, so that there is something to see all the year?

Regrettably, there are few broad-leaved evergreen trees hardy enough for much of the British Isles. For exposed sites, there is the

---

Above: Lapageria rosea 'Nash Court', an outstanding climber for a warm sheltered spot
Below: Prunus laurocerasus 'Otto Luyken' can double as ground cover or as a striking specimen shrub

common holm oak which, though a rather sombre deep green, has a nicely satisfying rounded shape. The common holly and many of its cultivars are also hardy, but tend to be slow-growing in exposed situations. Conifers are, of course, a natural for specimen status, particularly where a formal pyramid or a narrow spire is appropriate; *Abies delavayi* and *Cupressus glabra* are good in this capacity. Where some wind shelter is to be had, several quite majestic broad-leaved evergreens can be tried. Noteworthy are *Trachycarpus fortunei*, *Magnolia grandiflora*, *Garrya elliptica*, *Prunus laurocerasus* 'Magnoliifolia' and *Eucalyptus gunnii* and *E. niphophila*. Where milder conditions prevail, the choice is wider, encompassing such trees as *Embothrium*, *Drimys winteri* and *Cordyline australis*.

AGAINST WALLS AND FENCES

A highly acceptable artifice of garden design is to blend or marry the house with the garden. This is best accomplished by using wall shrubs or climbers on the house walls and smaller shrubs at their feet, leading away into the garden proper via linking features such as shrub beds or borders, internal hedges, or free-standing walls and fences planted with the same shrubs and climbers. Here again, the liberal use of evergreens will ensure that the whole planting scheme gladdens the eye from January to December.

Shrubs which grow well close against a wall, or respond to being trained flat upon it are termed wall shrubs. Often, plants which would be tender in your area can be grown in this way – *Ceanothus* and *Fremontodendron*, for example, in the colder parts of the British Isles – as a wall gives good frost-protection. Whether hardy or tender, there is plenty of choice (see also p. 63). If true climbers are preferred, there is a lot to be said for those that are self-clinging, obviating the need for wall nails or bolts and wires.

Among evergreen self-climbers that deserve to be seen more often are *Trachelospermum* and *Pileostegia*. The ivies should not be spurned, especially some of the variegated and less vigorous cultivars of *Hedera helix*.

OVER PERGOLAS, ARBOURS, SHRUBS AND TREES

Climbers need not, of course, be restricted to house walls and they are essential for clothing pergolas, arches and arbours. In such situations, evergreens are seldom used, with the exception of the semi-evergreen roses and Japanese honeysuckle. There are, however, several desirable sorts, including *Stauntonia hexaphylla* and *Holboellia coriacea*.

In the wild, climbers use trees and shrubs for support and the combination can be most effective. In the garden, host trees or shrubs and climbers must be chosen with care. Not only should the two associate well together, but the climber must not be too rampant or the host will be swamped. In general, it is best to select a fairly common tree or shrub as host, especially for the more vigorous climbers, and ideally one that is reasonably deep-rooted and has a fairly open branch system. A mixture of evergreen and deciduous shrubs can be very successful and the latter also gain some winter interest. Some of the most suitable climbers for this partnership are deciduous or herbaceous, for instance *Clematis macropetala* and *Tropaeolum speciosum*, which both look splendid when climbing up a holly or yew. Fully or moderately hardy evergreen climbers are rather few, but *Clematis cirrhosa* and especially its smaller-growing variety *balearica*, is one of the best. Among the half-hardies are *Berberidopsis*, *Asteranthera*, *Lapageria* and *Mitraria*, all very choice plants.

Like many Californian lilacs, *Ceanothus* × *veitchianus* is an excellent wall shrub

Photinia makes an eye-catching hedge

AS GROUND COVER

Low-growing evergreen shrubs are perfect as ground cover, keeping the soil surface covered at all times, including winter, when certain weeds will germinate during mild spells. Ground cover should not be divorced from the general planting scheme, but should be considered along with the main plants. Chosen with care, it can greatly enhance the overall effect (see also p. 62).

AS HEDGES AND WINDBREAKS

In open situations, the presence of a hedge or taller barrier to the windward can make all the difference to the environment of a garden. Shelter increases the range of plants one can grow well and ensures that the garden is a pleasant place in which to work, walk or sit. Deciduous trees and shrubs, especially if pruned or clipped to make them dense, are good wind filters. Evergreens are usually even more efficient, particularly in winter, and have the added advantage of providing a living backdrop of green throughout the year. A garden with evergreen hedges is a much more enticing place in winter than one surrounded by a leafless barrier.

Although hedges are windbreaks, the word is generally reserved for a much taller barrier of trees or large shrubs. Such conifers as pine, spruce, fir, cypress, arbor vitae and yew are often chosen, mainly because they are the hardiest and fastest-growing evergreen trees in northern Europe. If broad-leaved trees are

12

Hebe speciosa, a good medium-sized shrub for a container

preferred, then common holly and holm oak have much to commend them, although they are slower-growing. Cherry laurel is also good when allowed to grow with minimal pruning. Where frosts are less severe, there is more choice. Particularly satisfying are *Pittosporum*, *Hoheria sexstylosa* and *Drimys winteri* (see also p. 62).

EMBELLISHING THE PATIO AND COLD GREENHOUSE

From previous comments, it will be apparent that the fully hardy broad-leaved evergreens are outnumbered by those which are sensitive to severe frost. In the milder parts of the British Isles, the latter usually survive if planted in sheltered sites but, in the colder areas, they are generally too chancy anywhere outside.

A popular solution is to grow the tender species in containers. For much of the year, they can grace the edge of a broad drive, a patio or terrace and, when bad weather threatens, they can be housed in a shed or garage. Even better is to put the containerized plants in a cold greenhouse from late autumn until late spring. Some plants treated in this way, for example, *Lapageria rosea* and *Hebe speciosa* and its hybrids, will still be blooming when brought into the greenhouse and can be expected to continue for some time afterwards. Others, notably *Mahonia lomariifolia*, *Daphne odora* and *Clematis cirrhosa* var. *balearica*, normally flower in winter and will be at their best where they are most easily enjoyed. Artificial heat should not be necessary except in severe spells.

Cultivation

PLANTING AND MAINTENANCE

Most of the plants mentioned in this book are easily grown in Mr Everyman's garden and soil. Shelter from strong winds is, of course, beneficial but seldom essential, except where very low temperatures also prevail. Poor or very sharply drained soils are less satisfactory than average or moisture-retentive ones, but they can easily be improved. Unless a bed or border is being started from scratch, it is not usually necessary to dig the whole area. It is important, however, to prepare each planting hole thoroughly.

Dig a hole larger than the rootball and work into the bottom some well rotted manure, garden compost, leafmould or peat. If only the latter is used, add a sprinkling of general fertilizer. When planting a tree which is large enough to need support, knock a stake into the bottom of the hole. As the soil is returned to the hole around the plant, add some more organic matter. Firm well, leaving a very shallow depression to facilitate watering. Finish off with a light dressing of general fertilizer.

Although October and November, March and April are the best planting months, containerized plants can go in at any time if the weather is mild and the soil not wet or frozen. Make sure that the plants do not lack water during the first season and in dry spells give a thorough soaking once a week. In subsequent years, little attention is required. Only on the thinner and drier soils is it necessary to water, feed or mulch regularly. If growth is not satisfactory the second year, then a dressing of general fertilizer in late winter and a mulch of organic matter in late spring usually do the trick. Pruning or clipping should not be needed. However, if growth is thin, cutting back the leading stems by half in spring should promote branching. Most evergreens tolerate pruning if they get too big. Hedges and small windbreaks can be clipped in spring and late summer.

HARDINESS FACTORS

Hardy plants are capable of taking any weather likely to be

Evergreens in a garden in January

Fatsia japonica is frost-hardy, but needs protection from strong winds

experienced, but now and then winter cold is exceptionally severe and even some so-called hardy plants get damaged. Less hardy plants are those which are damaged by cold of lesser intensity. Much, of course, depends on where one lives in the British Isles. As all gardeners will know, the southern and western regions have the

16

mildest winters, the central and northeastern the coldest. In addition, coasts are less cold than several miles inland. This is the overall situation, but local topography and shelter from trees, hedges, walls and fences can make a profound difference. Even in the coldest area, a south-facing house wall with shelter from east winds will allow dubiously hardy plants to be grown.

Temperatures just below freezing combined with strong winds can be just as fatal, if not more so. This is because the strong bending movements caused by the wind squeeze the plant tissue, pushing the tiny sharp ice crystals into cell walls and rupturing them. Sudden thawing can have a similar effect, hence the usual recommendation not to place the more tender plants against east walls where they receive direct early morning sun after a frosty night.

The sap in cell tissue contains sugars and starches which lower the temperature at which it freezes. After a good warm summer, the current season's growth contains a higher percentage of sugars and thus provides greater frost-protection. If the summer has been dull and cool, sap sugars can be artificially boosted by dressing the soil with sulphate of potash at ⅓ oz per 10 sq. ft (10 g per m²). Lack of this summer ripening is the reason why some plants from continental climates – where summers are hotter and winters colder than ours – fail to thrive, regularly getting damaged in winter.

PESTS AND DISEASES

Most evergreens are remarkably free of pests and diseases. Aphids (greenfly and blackfly) may attack soft shoot tips and leaves and occasionally red spider mite may be a nuisance on wall shrubs and climbers, causing leaf mottling and defoliation. Of diseases, honey fungus is the deadliest, leading to the death of branches or of whole plants. Remedies for most of these troubles can be obtained at garden centres. Always follow the makers' instructions.

PROPAGATION

Many evergreens in all categories are fairly easy to propagate with a minimum of specialized knowledge. For those with no previous experience of propagating plants, *Plant Propagation* by Philip McMillan Browse (one of several volumes in the RHS *Encyclopaedia of Practical Gardening* series) is highly recommended. The main methods, in order of easiness and success rate, are layering, suckers, cuttings and seed.

Trees

Trees can be a splendid addition to the garden scene, but only if there is space for them to grow naturally and not look cramped. It is fair to say that any garden of 1/16 acre (250 m²) or less is best without a tree. Above this, two or three small trees or one of medium size is about right. Only in gardens of ½ acre (2,000 m²) or more will large trees look in keeping.

Apart from a small specimen in the large lawn or shrub bed to add height, trees should be situated towards the boundaries of a property, where they can be admired in their entirety and not as a backdrop. But consider the effect they may have on neighbours.

How big is a tree? For the purposes of this book, a small tree is 23 ft (7 m) tall at maturity, or approximately 20–25 years of age, a medium-sized tree is about 40 ft (12 m), and a large one around 65 ft (20 m). Of course, ultimate heights can be more or less, much depending on soil and situation. Generally speaking, a tree has a single stem or trunk for at least the lower third of its overall height and a head of branches developing above this level.

Many potentially large trees are especially decorative when young, for example, certain *Eucalyptus* and most conifers. Where room is at a premium for larger trees, there is something to be said for considering them as an expendable crop. A tree is planted, enjoyed until it fills its allotted space, then removed and replaced; or, if it will sprout from the base as some eucalypts will, it is cut down to ground level and a young shoot selected to take its place.

Abies (fir) Among the 40 known species of fir are several excellent accent trees. All are typified by the pyramidal or spire-like conifer shape and a central main stem bearing whorls of horizontal branches, clad with needle-like leaves. The best small species is undoubtedly *Abies koreana* (see p. 26). Not only is it slow-growing, but it produces its attractive violet-purple cones when quite young. Even without cones, the dark green foliage, blue-white beneath, demands attention. It can be particularly effective surrounded by winter heath, *Erica carnea*. Somewhat larger but of equal merit is

Arbutus × andrachnoides can eventually grow to 30 ft (9 m) and is a fine specimen tree

A. delavayi, with larger, barrel-shaped, deep purple cones. Hardiest are var. *georgei*, with hairy stems, and var. *forrestii*, which has orange shoots and conspicuous white winter buds. All are best in acid soils.

Acacia (wattle) None of the 1,200 acacias is fully hardy, but a few of the Australian species are well worth trying in mild areas. Best known is the silver wattle, *Acacia dealbata*, aptly named for its silvery grey, elegantly ferny foliage and spring-borne trusses of small, yellow, pompon-like flowerheads which are fragrant – the florists' mimosa. It is a large tree and fast-growing, but flowers young and is expendable if it doesn't succumb first to a hard winter. Many wattles and certainly most of the hardier species dispense with leaf blades and produce flattened leaf stalks known as phyllodes. In *A. longifolia*, the Sydney golden wattle, these phyllodes are just like willow-shaped leaves, while in *A. pravissima* they are curiously like the centre-board of a yacht and set vertically on the twigs. Both make small slender trees, *A. longifolia* producing cylindrical flower spikes and *A. pravissima* showers of tiny pompons, both in bright yellow and in spring. Although best in a neutral to acid soil, these two will stand some lime.

Arbutus (strawberry tree) Rich green glossy foliage, clusters of engaging, urn-shaped, white flowers and spherical red to orange fruits – not really much like strawberries – make this a very desirable genus. Only one species grows fast enough to be considered a tree in the 25-year period. This is the western North American madrona, *Arbutus menziesii*, which in time becomes a large tree with leaves up to 4 in. (10 cm) or more long and smooth cinnamon-red bark of great appeal. The common strawberry tree, *A. unedo*, is rarely more than 20 ft (6 m) tall and has smaller leaves but showier flowers and brighter fruits, produced together in autumn and winter. It is often grown as a large shrub and, being fairly slow-growing, is good in this role. The pink-flowered form, *rubra*, is well worth seeking. Rather similar is the hybrid *A. × andrachnoides* (*unedo × andrachne*), which has the added attraction of smooth and peeling reddish bark (see p. 18). Both it and *A. unedo* prefer a neutral to acid soil.

Azara About half the species in this genus will make small trees 16–20 ft (5–6 m) in height. They are not fully hardy but, though the young stems may be frosted, growth quickly appears lower down. All are comparatively graceful, with small glossy leaves in frond-like sprays. Yellow, petalless and fragrant flowers occur in axillary clusters in late winter or spring. Hardiest is *Azara microphylla*, with deep green, toothed leaves about ½–1 in. (1–2.5 cm) long and very small, bright yellow flowers. It tolerates some lime in the soil.

Ceanothus (Californian lilac; see also p. 30) Very few of the evergreen ceanothus species achieve tree status and those that do need sheltered sites. Both *Ceanothus arboreus* and *C. thyrsiflorus* can reach 26–33 ft (8–10 m) in height in favourable positions and, when smothered in pale blue flowers in early spring to early summer, they are a sight to behold. The latter, in particular, is handsome at all times, with its oval, boldly veined, deep lustrous green foliage and bushy habit. Both will perform well in limy soils.

Chamaecyparis (false cypress) The false cypresses are distinguished from the true cypresses, *Cupressus* (p. 22), by their flattened stems and scale-leaves arranged in frond-like two-dimensional sprays. All are narrowly pyramidal to columnar and make good accent plants. Most are potentially large but not especially fast-growing and are easily cut down when too big. All are happy where lime is present in the soil. The Lawson cypress, *Chamaecyparis lawsoniana*, is the best known and more than 200 cultivars have been recorded. They differ in vigour, habit and especially in foliage colour, from bright yellow and gold to blue-green and white-variegated. Recommended are 'Stewartii', yellow (see p. 26); 'Blue Jacket', blue-grey; 'Allumii', grey, broadly columnar; and 'Grayswood Pillar', grey, very narrowly columnar. The Nootka cypress, *C. nootkatensis*, is the most elegant, being more pyramidal until older, with pendent branchlets. It tends to be faster-growing then *C. lawsoniana* and is a darker green. Intriguing in outline is the slower-growing cultivar 'Pendula'. It has whole branches hanging almost vertically in the best weeping-willow tradition, but the effect can be rather gaunt as the tree ages.

Cordyline (New Zealand cabbage tree) Familiar when small as an accent plant among colourful annuals, *Cordyline australis* can, in time, reach 20–33 ft (6–10 m) or more in height. Until it attains flowering size, it forms a pole-like stem topped by a dense rosette of strap-shaped leaves up to 3 ft (1 m) long. After the large airy trusses of fragrant, white, starry flowers have been produced, the stem forks into two or three branches. These in turn elongate, flower and fork, building up an open head of robust branches. In the milder south and west, it develops into a small, somewhat palm-like tree of

In colder areas, *Drimys winteri* can be grown as a large wall shrub

great character, flowering regularly in early summer each year and producing small white berries which add interest until the winter. It seems happy in all soil types.

Crinodendron The Chilean lantern tree, *Crinodendron hookerianum* (*Tricuspidaria lanceolata*), is another unreliably hardy plant, which takes time to reach 10 ft (3 m) or more and needs shelter, shade, acid soil and a good rainfall. The deep green, willowy leaves are a little sombre in tone, but are a perfect foil for the long-stemmed, pendent, crimson, urn-shaped flowers, which appear in early summer. It can equally be grown as a large shrub. (See p. 26.)

Cupressus (true cypress) This genus of about 20 coniferous tree species from the northern hemisphere is characterized by its slender, rounded, freely branching stems, clad with tiny scale-leaves in three-dimensional sprays (see also *Chamaecyparis*, p. 21). They are pyramidal to columnar trees, usually fairly fast-growing and thriving in well drained soils. The best of these for the smaller garden is *Cupressus glabra* 'Pyramidalis' (*C. arizonica* var. *glabra* 'Pyramidalis'). It forms mossy pyramids of smoky grey foliage of great appeal and the trunk and main branches have smooth, peeling, reddish bark. It reaches about 65 ft (20 m) in height and is only moderate in speed of growth.

Drimys (winter's bark) Given shelter from freezing winds, *Drimys winteri*, a small to medium-sized South American species, can make an eye-catchingly lush, broad-leaved specimen tree for all soils. It is variable in habit, some forms bushing out from the base, others looking more tree-like, though both grow as tall. The foliage too differs somewhat according to soil and situation. The aromatic, substantial, glossy leaves are more or less elliptic, 5–8 in. (12–20 cm) long, always with a blue-white patina beneath, but varying from deep to pale or almost yellow-green above. In spring, long-stalked pendent umbels of fragrant, creamy white flowers appear, having been held in fat red buds all the winter. But for the irregular number of rather narrow petals, the flowers could be mistaken for cherry. Severe winters can reduce this handsome tree to a bare trunk or main branches, but it has remarkable powers of recovery.

Embothrium (Chilean fire tree or bush) *Embothrium coccineum* is a truly spectacular evergreen tree when loaded with clusters of its curiously shaped, tubular, crimson flowers in May and June. It needs acid soil and is not always easy to get established.

Eucalyptus (gum tree) Most *Eucalyptus* species have two sorts of foliage, juvenile and adult. In general, the adult leaves are narrowly to broadly lance-shaped and carried alternately. Juvenile leaves vary greatly from species to species, but are much broader and borne in opposite pairs. They are often richly grey-green to blue-white and very ornamental; the juvenile foliage of *E. gunnii*, for example, is much used in the floristry trade. By regular cutting back each spring, either to ground level or to the top of a leg or trunk, juvenile foliage can be maintained indefinitely. Easily available and reasonably hardy is the Tasmanian *E. gunnii*, which is known as cider gum. It has small, blue-white, rounded juvenile leaves and grey-green lance-shaped adult ones. It can in time get large, but may be easily kept to size by pruning, or can be replaced by young plants. Undoubtedly the hardiest of all the gums and, for that reason alone, deserving of much greater popularity is the snow gum, *E. niphophila* (now *E. pauciflora* subsp. *niphophila*). Further points in its favour are its small tree size, slow growth (for a eucalypt) and handsome flaking bark, creating a mosaic of creams, browns, greys and near-reds. Both the juvenile and adult leaves may be green or a shade of grey.

Eucalypts must be planted young before they can get pot-bound. Once the roots are tightly wound around in a pot, they never seem to radiate outwards when finally planted and all too often the tree

Eucryphia × *nymansensis* flowers best with its head in the sun and the roots shady and cool

blows over in a gale. The best approach is to sow seed in warmth in late winter, prick off the seedlings singly as soon as large enough to handle, harden them off and plant out at about the end of May. The resulting trees will be 3–6½ ft (1–2 m) high by autumn.

Eucryphia Glossy, deep green leaves contrast marvellously with white or cream flowers, especially if the latter are of good size and centred with an elegant puff of gold-tipped stamens. Such a combination occurs in *Eucryphia*, notably the hybrid *E.* × *nymansensis*. This has a columnar habit eventually up to 33 ft (10 m) or more in height, pinnate leaves and pure white flowers 2½ in. (6 cm) across in late summer. Although fairly hardy, it responds to shelter and partial shade and must have neutral to acid soil.

Ilex (holly; see also p. 35) No garden should be without at least one holly and there are lots to choose from among the 400 species and numerous cultivars. Several grow into trees and much could be said for the very familiar common holly, *Ilex aquifolium*, or one of its strikingly variegated cultivars. Superior in leaf size and effectiveness in a garden setting is its hybrid, *I.* × *altaclerensis*. One of the best of this group is 'Hodginsii', sometimes sold simply as *I.* × *altaclerensis*, which has purplish stems and large, mainly non-spiny, lustrous leaves. It is male (hollies have male and female flowers on separate plants), so if berries are required, it must be planted near a female such as 'Camelliifolia'. This has equally good foliage, not

Ilex × *koehneana* 'Chestnut Leaf' has glossy spiny leaves 6 in. (15 cm) or more long

unlike that of its namesake camellia, glossy, spineless and sometimes up to 5 in. (13 cm) in length. Really eye-catching is the variegated 'Lawsoniana', with each leaf blade boldly and centrally blotched bright gold and yellow-green. Equally tree-like and deserving to be more widely grown is another hybrid, *I.* × *koehneana*, which arose as a cross between *I. aquifolium* and the large-leaved *I. latifolium*. 'Chestnut Leaf' is a fine named seedling.

Laurus The common bay or sweet laurel, *Laurus nobilis*, is all too often seen as a topiary specimen, or kept pruned as a bush. It responds well to pruning and regular removal of the strongest leading stem tips in spring will maintain a pleasing informal shape. Given headroom, however, bay soon becomes a small to medium-sized tree, although it can be cut back by really severe winters. It is perhaps a little sombre for some tastes, but this criticism cannot be levelled at the cultivar 'Aurea', which is golden green throughout the year and brightest while the young leaves unfurl. Bay flowers in spring, producing in the leaf axils small blooms composed mainly of creamy stamens. Viewed *en masse*, the fluffy clusters are modestly pretty. All well drained soils are acceptable.

Magnolia Frequently grown as a wall shrub, *Magnolia grandiflora* or bull bay is an evergreen tree *par excellence*. It is surprisingly hardy in a sheltered site and has a height potential of 33 ft (10 m). When young, its oval, 5–10 in. (13–25 cm) long leaves are felted with

red-brown hair, but they soon become dark green with a good gloss. The magnificent, bowl-shaped, creamy white flowers are carried fairly sparingly from late summer to late autumn and always excite comment. In the largest-flowered cultivar, 'Goliath', they can be 10 in. (25 cm) in diameter. Bull bay needs a fertile moisture-retentive soil, but is lime-tolerant. (See p. 4.)

Quercus (oak) Among the 600 species of oak, there are many evergreens, but few are really frost-hardy. The common evergreen or holm oak, *Quercus ilex*, is surprisingly fast-growing when young, even in poor soils, provided it does not lack adequate moisture, and is medium to large when mature. Similar is the less hardy cork oak, *Q. suber*, its rippling waves of corky bark an added attraction. Var. *occidentalis* is hardier, but it has a less dramatic bark. Tailor-made for the smaller garden is *Q. phillyreoides* from China and Japan. It has oval leaves 1¼–2½ in. (3–6 cm) long, which are a rich bright green above and paler beneath. It tends to stay as a large bush and needs the lower branches removed (a few at a time each year in early spring) to build up a single tree-like stem.

Trachycarpus (windmill or Chusan fan palm) *Trachycarpus fortunei* is the only palm hardy enough to stand British winters away from the known mild areas. It has a straight trunk, which looks as though it is covered with shaggy, dark brown, coconut matting, and a fairly compact head of pleated fan-shaped leaves 2–4 ft (60–120 cm) long. A well grown specimen can attain 33 ft (10 m) in height, but takes many years to do so. When old enough, it produces big arching trusses of tiny yellow flowers each summer. Chusan palm will grow in alkaline and acid soils.

Umbellularia (California laurel, headache tree) Surprisingly hardy considering its Californian homeland, *Umbellularia californica* is a member of the laurel family and can attain the proportions of a small tree in sheltered sites. In California, it becomes much bigger. Erect-growing in its early years, it has distinctively yellow-green, willow-shaped leaves and tufty flower clusters reminiscent of those of *Laurus nobilis*. The strong, sweetly pungent scent which the whole tree gives off on a warm day or when bruised can cause a headache if inhaled for too long, hence its common name.

Above: Abies koreana (left) can provide an attractive focal point; the Chusan palm *(right)* needs shelter from freezing winds
Below: the yellow Lawson cypress 'Stewartii' set off by *Juniperus squamata* 'Meyeri' *(left)*; the desirable *Crinodendron hookerianum (right)*

Large Shrubs

Although the largest shrubs can equal small trees in stature, they lack a single stem or trunk, branching from below to just above ground level. When well developed, they form a conspicuous and solid shape which should be turned to advantage. In the small garden, for example under ⅟₁₆ acre (250 m²) in extent, one or two large shrubs can be used as a focal point instead of a small tree. Elsewhere, they should be planted in key positions, either to add height to a shrub or mixed bed or border, or as a background for smaller and choicer things. Some of the less hardy ones are excellent wall shrubs.

All the shrubs described below can attain at least 10 ft (3 m) in height, though some may take many years to achieve it. Among their ranks is a wide variety of habits and foliage types. Several also bloom splendidly, being hard to rival for the profligacy and richness of their floral displays.

Arundinaria (bamboo) The elegance and easy-going nature of most hardy bamboos make them an ideal subject for the modern garden. At last this message seems to have got through and bamboos in general are steadily increasing in popularity. *Arundinaria* provides some of the best examples, noteworthy being *A. murieliae* (of gardens). Densely clump-forming and usually less than 13 ft (4 m) tall, its smooth green canes have a waxy white patina at the nodes and the willow-shaped leaves a charming tesselated vein pattern. *Arundinaria nitida* (now *Sinarundinaria nitida*) is sometimes confused with it, but the canes often have a glossy purple flush. Any well drained, not dry soil is acceptable.

Berberis (barberry; see also p. 43) Some of the large evergreen barberries also happen to be among the finest in the genus. Very familiar but undoubtedly the best for garden-worthiness is *Berberis darwinii*. With its pleasing arching habit, tiny, deep green, holly-like leaves and profusion of golden-orange flowers, it is a sight to behold in spring. *Berberis × stenophylla*, the hybrid with *B. empetrifolia*

With its green-and-white leaves and interesting flowers, *Feijoa sellowiana* is a fine, large, bushy shrub

(p. 53) is also good, but its vigorous suckering habit can be a nuisance. The choicest species by far is *B. valdiviana*. When well established, it has a columnar habit up to 10 ft (3 m) high, covered with glossy, almost spineless leaves up to 3 in. (8 cm) long. In late spring and early summer, pendent chains of saffron-yellow flowers garland the twigs, contrasting beautifully with the rich green leaves. Despite its southern Chilean homeland, *B. valdiviana* is perfectly hardy except in winters of continental severity. Reasonably fertile soils, both acid and alkaline, are suitable.

Ceanothus (Californian lilac) Both species described in the Trees chapter (p. 21) can be grown as large shrubs and are often treated in this way. Also highly attractive is *Ceanothus impressus*, with its fish-bone mode of branching and abundant deep blue flowers in early summer. Its foliage too has great appeal, each tiny, deep green, rounded leaf blade being ¼ – ½ in. (6–12 mm) long, almost convex in cross section, with a deeply impressed vein pattern – hence its specific name. For late summer and autumn flowering, *C.* 'Autumnal Blue' takes some beating. Somewhat similar to its parent, *C. thyrsiflorus*, it bears much richer blue flowers and is of lesser stature though still tall, especially on a wall. Also derived from *C. thyrsiflorus* and perhaps only a form of it is *C.* 'Cascade', with elegantly arching branches and powder-blue flowers in early summer. Many other fine, large-growing, Californian lilacs are available, notable being *C. dentatus* and *C.* × *veitchianus* (p. 45), *C. cyaneus* and *C.* 'Russellianus'. All well drained, reasonably fertile soils are acceptable, even those over chalk, and a sheltered sunny position is essential.

Cephalotaxus (plum-fruited yew) The majority of conifers are either sizable trees or lowish shrubs and very few come into the large shrub category. *Cephalotaxus harringtonia* var. *drupacea* is one of the exceptions, a pleasing and fairly slow-growing, spreading shrub seldom above 10 ft (3 m) tall. In foliage it much resembles a magnified yew, the narrow, leathery, semi-glossy leaves being up to 2 in. (5 cm) or more in length. Unlike the yew, the fruits are plum-like, with the single seed completely enclosed in a rather hard, fibrous flesh. Unfortunately, *C. harringtonia* is dioecious, that is, the male and female flowers are borne on separate plants, and so one needs a bush of each to see these curious, uncone-like fruits. The cultivar 'Fastigiata' has the erect habit of a young Irish yew and has very dark green foliage. It makes an unusual specimen for the smaller lawn. Most garden soils are suitable and quite deep shade is tolerated.

Cotoneaster Among the 50 known species in this genus are several valuable garden plants, one of which is *Cotoneaster lacteus*, originally introduced from western China in 1913. It has an attractive arching mode of growth and takes some years to reach 10 ft (3 m). The deep matt-green, oval leaves are white- to yellowish-felted beneath, the two colours contrasting interestingly on a windy day. In summer, flattish clusters of white flowers appear, to be followed by deep red berries, which do not colour until late in the year and persist until the following spring. Less arching and more spreading is *C. salicifolius*. This has willow-like, brighter green leaves, which are more or less white-hairy beneath. It flowers earlier and has lighter, brighter fruits, which ripen sooner and are more prone to be eaten by birds. Cotoneasters are amenable to almost all soils and conditions.

Daphniphyllum In foliage, the Japanese *Daphniphyllum macropodum* resembles a rhododendron. It has a full and rounded habit, plentifully clad with oval leaves up to 6 in. (15 cm) or even more in length. They are generally a rich, almost lustrous green above, grey-blue beneath and carried on conspicuously red stalks. Quite unlike those of a rhododendron are the pale green, tufty flower clusters which open in the leaf axils in spring. It makes a handsome foliage plant and will tolerate some lime in the soil.

Desfontainia Chile seems to have the monopoly of choice evergreens with showy red flowers. One of the hardiest and equal in beauty to *Crinodendron* (p. 22) is *Desfontainia spinosa*. Basically holly-like but with softer prickles, it bears in summer and early autumn a succession of scarlet and yellow, pendent, tubular flowers of great charm. It is slow-growing and needs a sheltered site in neutral to acid soil. It thrives best in areas of high rainfall with mild winters, but will stand short spells of quite severe frosts.

Elaeagnus (oleaster) The hardy evergreen members of this genus all have garden value as foliage plants and some are particularly good. Perhaps the best is the Japanese and Korean *Elaeagnus macrophylla*, having a rounded habit and bold appearance when well grown. The deep lustrous green, rounded to elliptic leaves can be 4 in. (10 cm) long and have a silvery pearly sheen beneath, which almost flashes as the leaves are turned in a strong wind. In autumn, small, silvery white, pendent, fragrant flowers appear in the leaf

'Frederici', another variegated cultivar of *Elaeagnus pungens*, with pale yellow markings on the leaves

axils. Sometimes they are followed by red berry-like fruits spangled with tiny rusty scales. Slower-growing and less spreading in habit is *E. pungens*. It has narrower leaves, the whitish undersides of which are enlivened by a sprinkling of red-brown scales. In gardens, its startlingly gold-splashed cultivar, 'Maculata', is more commonly met with. On dull winter days, it really lights up its particular garden niche. There is also 'Gilt Edge', a newer cultivar with a broad yellow margin to the leaf. All these oleasters are suitable for most soils and grow well near the sea.

Euonymus (spindle tree) Japanese spindle, *Euonymus japonicus*, is best known as a hedging shrub, especially in maritime districts. Allowed to grow naturally, it can eventually reach 10 ft (3 m) and form a handsome garden feature with its glossy, rich green, oval, leathery leaves. The flowers are insignificant but, when produced in quantity, the pinkish seed pods and orange-coated seeds are intriguing. For those who like variegated foliage there are several noteworthy cultivars. The spindles thrive in most ordinary soils.

Fatsia (false castor-oil plant) *Fatsia japonica*, widely grown as a long-suffering houseplant, may be planted outside in a site sheltered from strong cold winds and steadily builds up into one of the finest of all large-leaved foliage plants. Each leaf is long-stalked, the lustrous leathery blade up to 1 ft (30 cm) long and wide and divided into several finger-like lobes. Well into autumn, quite large terminal clusters of small milk-white flowers open, to be followed, if the winter is mild, by pea-sized black berries which ripen in spring. 'Variegata' has white tips to the leaf lobes, but this is hardly an improvement. *Fatsia japonica* is a natural specimen shrub and looks splendid underplanted with spring bulbs. It grows well near the sea and in most soils and tolerates shade. (See p. 16.)

Feijoa Only in areas of warm summers and mild winters is one likely to see the oval, green, red-flushed fruits of this attractive guava ally, *Feijoa sellowiana*. Even so, the shrub needs no more than its leaves and flowers to be desirable. White-felted stems bear pairs of oval, deep green leaves with a white-felted reverse. In summer, fascinating flowers unfold from the leaf axils. Each one has four curiously cupped petals, whitish without and crimson-flushed within, and a central brush of gold-tipped, deep crimson stamens. Considering that central South America is the homeland of this large shrub, it is surprisingly hardy, but it must have the protection of a sunny wall in colder areas. (See p. 28.)

Fremontodendron Sometimes called *Fremontia*, *Fremontodendron* is best known as a provider of several spectacular wall shrubs, though where frost is not too severe they quickly become small trees. As wall shrubs, they can be grown in all but the coldest areas and stand up to quite hard pruning. The lobed leaves are rather maple-like, semi-glossy deep green above and grey with a layer of tiny star-shaped hairs beneath. These hairs also clothe young shoots, are easily rubbed off and take to the air. They can act as a highly efficient itching powder and must be kept out of the eyes at all costs. 'California Glory' is the best of the bunch for hardiness and floral profusion, and a truly garden-worthy plant. (See p. 34.)

Garrya Although a native of California and southern Oregon, *Garrya elliptica* is a very successful hardy shrub in much of the British Isles. It is a somewhat sombre but nevertheless appealing evergreen for much of the year and in winter it lights up with quantities of silky, silvery grey catkins up to 8 in. (20 cm) in length. This is the usually planted male tree. The female has smaller tighter catkins and, if a male is nearby, these develop into fat chains of silky-hairy, purple-brown, berry-like fruits, which always intrigue gardeners who have not seen them before. The male cultivar, 'James Roof', from California is said to produce catkins up to 13 in. (35 cm) in length, but such excess seems to be curbed in Britain. Although normally grown as a wall shrub, *G. elliptica* looks even

Fremontodendron 'California Glory' is covered in large, glowing yellow flowers throughout the summer

better as a free-standing specimen surrounded by lawn and can be seen to great effect in this way at the Cambridge Botanic Garden. All well drained soils are acceptable and half-day shade tolerated.

Hoheria (lacebark, houhere) Two members of this New Zealand genus could have been included in the Trees chapter, but only in mild areas can they be expected to get so big. Generally, they provide very pleasing wall shrubs with just that touch of class. Hardiest is *Hoheria sexstylosa*, its slender stems clad in lance-shaped, sharply toothed, semi-glossy leaves 2–7 in. (5–18 cm) long. These provide the perfect foil for a foam of white blossom in late summer. *Hoheria populnea* has the best foliage, being glossier, broader and more boldly toothed. The floral display is equally good. The cultivar 'Variegata' has greenish yellow leaves with a deep green margin, while 'Alba Variegata' has deep green foliage irregularly margined white and often pink-tinted when young. There is also 'Purpurea', with deep purple undersides to the leaves, but a commercial source is hard to find. Most fertile soils are suitable.

The striking flowers of *Itea ilicifolia* appear in late summer and early autumn

Ilex (holly) All the large hollies discussed in the Trees chapter (p. 24) can be grown as big shrubs, tolerating pruning if this becomes necessary. In addition, there are several hollies which merit a place in the garden more often than they are seen. *Ilex fargesii* can in time make a small tree, but large shrub is its general *forte*. Like many of the Asiatic species, it is very un-holly-like in having oblanceolate (inversely lance-shaped), spineless, few-toothed, dark green leaves 2–5 in. (5–13 cm) long. The bright red berries can be showy when produced in quantity. The same general comments can be made about *I. pedunculosa*, but here the smooth oval leaves are even less like a holly and the red berries dangle from stalks like small cherries – a very atypical feature indeed. Most soils are suitable for these hollies.

Itea Conveniently following *Ilex* in the evergreen shrub index, *Itea ilicifolia* resembles a traditional holly in a remarkable way, although there is no botanical relationship. This shrub produces its tiny greenish white flowers in elegant catkins 6–12 in. (15–30 cm)

long and, despite a lack of definite colour, the floral display is decidedly eye-catching and would surely excite comment if it were seen more often. Curiously enough, *I. ilicifolia* is easily obtained commercially. Both alkaline and acid soils are suitable.

Juniperus (juniper; see also p. 47) Quite a few junipers are naturally of shrub size when mature. Readily available but not to be despised is *Juniperus squamata* 'Meyeri'. This Chinese cultivar has an erect to ascending habit of growth, often more or less oblong in outline, but always wayward enough to create a shrub of character. The densely borne, awl-shaped leaves are blue-green with a touch of silver and very effective in morning and evening light. It thrives in ordinary, well drained soil and sun. (See p. 26.)

Kalmia (see also p. 55) The mountain laurel, *Kalmia latifolia*, also known as calico bush in its native North America, is a shrub to rival the best rhododendrons when covered in bloom. For much of the year, its glossy green, 2–5 in. (5–13 cm) long, laurel-like leaves make it a desirable evergreen. In early summer, a transformation takes place when the stem tips light up with clusters of bright, pure pink blossom. Each flower is about ¾–1 in. (2–2.5 cm) in diameter and resembles an exquisitely designed, up-turned lampshade. A moist acid soil is absolutely essential for success.

Mahonia (see also p. 48) *Mahonia* differs from *Berberis* (p. 29) in lacking stem spines and having pinnately divided leaves; furthermore, the flowers spikes are clustered at the tips of the stems, making a greater floral impact. Definitely a tall shrub and eventually a small tree, but fairly slow-growing, is *M. lomariifolia*. Sparingly branched, erect and almost palm-like, each stem terminates in a wide rosette of leathery leaves, composed of 19 to 37 deep green, glossy, spiny-margined leaflets. These are the perfect foil for the fountain-like trusses of rich bright yellow, fragrant flowers, which open between autumn and spring. Unfortunately, this species is not very hardy and gets scorched or cut back in severe winters. It requires a neutral to acid soil to thrive. The commonly grown *M. bealei* and *M. japonica*, which are very similar to each other, are bushier and lower-growing than *M. lomariifolia*, taking many years to achieve 8–10 ft (2.5–3 m). The leaves have fewer larger leaflets and the flowers are a paler yellow. Although less spectacular in bloom than *M. lomariifolia*, the display is longer, starting in early autumn and finishing in late spring. Both are hardy and grow in most humus-rich soils, though on lime they may be a less satisfactory green. By crossing M. *japonica* with M. *lomariifolia*, a very handsome compromise has resulted – M. × *media* 'Charity'. This blends the parental characters to a nicety, having vigorous, bushy, bold foliage and showy flowers. Others worthy of mention are 'Winter Sun' and 'Lionel Fortescue'.

Olearia (daisy bush; see also p. 49) Among the one hundred or more species of *Olearia*, one stands out as a strikingly handsome large shrub. This is O. *macrodonta* from New Zealand. Superficially, the olive-grey leaves are rather holly-like, but the more numerous marginal spines are soft and the undersides are clad with a thin, white, felty layer. In summer, tiny, fragrant, daisy-like, white flowerheads open in largish flattened clusters. *Olearia ilicifolia* is closely related and has a similar appeal, but bears distinctively narrow leaves. Eventually and in areas of high rainfall it can attain 10 ft (3 m). Both grow in a wide variety of well drained, fertile soils and are fairly hardy, but can suffer in severe winters.

The crimped buds of *Kalmia latifolia* could be compared to icing on a cake

Phillyrea After an initial burst of growth, *Phillyrea latifolia* (*P. media*) is fairly slow-growing, to such an extent that it is usually grown as a large shrub rather than the small tree it can become. Of rounded habit and densely leafy, it makes a satisfying setting for choicer plants. In cultivation, this variable species is mainly represented by two distinct plants – the clone 'Rotundifolia', having broadly oval leaves ¾–2½ in. (2–6 cm) long, and the form *spinosa*, with narrower, sharply toothed blades. Tiny whitish flowers are borne in the leaf axils in late spring and are sometimes followed by blue-black berry-like fruits. Practically all soils and situations are acceptable.

Photinia From a foliage point of view, *Photinia* × *fraseri* 'Red Robin' resembles *Pieris formosa* var. *forrestii* 'Wakehurst' (below). The leaves are a little broader, but equally bright red when young. Unlike the pierises, which are members of the heather family, the photinias are allied to *Pyracantha* and *Cotoneaster* (rose family) and bear broad clusters of tiny, five-petalled, white flowers in early summer. Also unlike *Pieris*, *P.* × *fraseri* thrives in a wide spectrum of soils, including those that are chalky. Sun or partial shade are tolerated and a sheltered site gives the best results. (See p. 12.)

Pieris Like *Kalmia* and *Rhododendron*, this highly garden-worthy genus only thrives in moist acid soil and in sites sheltered from cold winds. For all gardens with such conditions, *Pieris formosa* var. *forrestii* is a must. Seldom less than 8 ft (2.5 m) eventually, and capable of 13 ft (4 m) in height, it has lance-shaped to elliptic leaves, 2½–6 in. (6–15 cm) long, which are deep lustrous green when mature. In late spring or early summer, the stem tips drip with large pendent clusters of slenderly urn-shaped, white flowers. At about the same time or a little later, clusters of young leaves appear which are a startling red and equally as bright as many flowers of this colour. In cultivation, the main clone of this type is 'Wakehurst', but several newer ones are also available, such as 'Forest Flame' and 'Firecrest', both reputedly of hybrid origin with *P. japonica* (p. 50).

Pittosporum (kohuhu) The New Zealand kohuhu, *Pittosporum tenuifolium*, is a decorative and useful seaside plant, either as a windbreak, clipped hedge, or solitary specimen. The foliage sprays, comprising slender black twigs and glossy, pale green, wavy, oval leaves, are widely used by florists and many acres of stooled plants are grown for this purpose. In spring, small chocolate-purple honey-scented flowers appear in the leaf axils. Although often overlooked, they are worthy of close appraisal. Kohuhu is erect and quick-growing. Away from the sea, it is prone to damage or death in severe winters, but makes a splendid pot or tub plant for the patio. There are several notable coloured-leaved cultivars. All tend to be more tender than the species. Any well drained soil is suitable.

Prunus (laurel; see also p. 56) Common cherry laurel, *Prunus laurocerasus*, is so often used for hedging or as a barrier that it tends to get forgotten as a specimen. For this latter purpose, the cultivar 'Magnoliifolia' is hard to better, with its 1 ft (30 cm) long, lustrous, oval leaves. It thrives best in shade and fairly soon builds up into a big shrub or even a small tree. Erect spikes of creamy white flowers open in spring and are followed by small bitter cherries, which change from green through red to glossy black-purple. The Portugal laurel, *P. lusitanica*, is also widely planted. Grown in shade, it develops the deepest green, oval leaves up to 5 in. (13 cm) long, the upper surface having an almost satiny sheen. The cultivar 'Variegata' has white-margined, smaller leaves and is less vigorous. Both laurels grow in most soils and are hardy, but leaves and stem tips may be damaged in severe wind frosts.

Pieris 'Forest Flame' tends to be neater and more compact in habit than 'Wakehurst'

Pyracantha (firethorn) Despite their undeniable hardiness, the firethorns are generally seen as wall shrubs. They are even better at the back of a border and can be used for hedging. *Pyracantha coccinea* 'Lalandei' is planted everywhere and it certainly is reliable, with its profusion of cream flowers around midsummer and bright orange-red fruits in autumn and winter. Having the advantage of large, more richly glossy leaves and scarlet fruits is *P. atalantioides*, although unfortunately it is susceptible to fireblight. *Pyracantha rogersiana*, *P. crenulata* and *P. crenato-serrata* offer variations on the theme, the latter having coarsely toothed leaves up to 3 in. (7.5 cm) in length. Well worth trying are some of the hybrid cultivars, such as 'Buttercup', yellow fruits; 'Orange Glow', bright orange fruits; and 'Shawnee', light orange fruits on disease-resistant bushy growth. All the firethorns are fast-growing and tolerant of a wide range of soil types.

Viburnum (see also p. 57) The best known evergreen viburnum is the laurustinus, *V. tinus*, a bushy shrub with semi-glossy oval leaves and conspicuous flattened clusters of small white flowers in winter and spring. It is ideal for seaside gardens and those protected from icy winds. In severe winters, leaves and stem tips may be scorched.

The flowers of *Pyracantha rogersiana* are followed by golden yellow to reddish orange berries

Var. *lucidum* has glossier leaves and the form *hirtulum* or *hirtum* is hairy. Of the cultivars, 'Purpureum' is particularly effective, with purple young leaves which darken as they mature and contrast well with the flowers. 'Variegatum' has creamy yellow-patterned foliage and is less hardy. 'Eve Price' is the best in flower, with carmine buds.

Very different is *Viburnum rhytidophyllum*. This has the longest leaves of all the hardy species, up to 8 in. (20 cm) when well grown. Each blade is narrowly oval, glossy and finely corrugated above and grey-felted beneath. In early summer, flattened heads of small white flowers open and are followed by red berries which mature shining black. It soon builds up into a large shrub, doing well even in dry shade. Crossed with the European wayfaring tree, *V. lantana*, it has given us *V. × rhytidophylloides*, a very vigorous and handsome hybrid much like its evergreen parent, but with shorter wider leaves. *Viburnum* 'Pragense' is another *rhytidophyllum* hybrid, this time with the small-leaved *V. utile*. It is a superb shrub, with dark green, 3–5 in. (7–13 cm) long, finely wrinkled leaves, which in shade take on an almost satiny lustre. In late spring, white flowers expand from pink buds. Although raised more than 30 years ago, it is only just becoming available from nurserymen.

The tall fast-growing *Viburnum × rhytidophylloides* can be useful as a screen

Medium-sized Shrubs

On the whole, shrubs of medium stature are the most useful of all, both for filling in the background and for providing focal points. Some of the more spectacular ones deserve specimen status at the edge of a lawn or the end of a path. All the shrubs described below can attain at least 6½ ft (2 m) in height, though some take several years to do so.

Abelia None of the evergreen abelias is totally hardy, but they are great providers of blossom and worthy of a place at the foot of a sheltered wall. *Abelia × grandiflora* has erect, later arching stems and forms a bushy shrub with bright deep green, oval leaves 1¼–2½ in. (3–6 cm) long. From midsummer to autumn, they are enlivened by a succession of ¾ in. (2 cm) long funnel-shaped flowers, which start pink-tinted and age white. There is a light fragrance. For those who like variegated foliage, the cultivars 'Francis Mason', 'Gold Strike', 'Goldspot' and 'Variegata' should be looked out for. The first-mentioned is particularly attractive. All grow well in most fertile soils, but need shelter from cold winds.

Aucuba The spotted form of *Aucuba japonica* is the most familiar and the best cultivars are 'Crotonifolia' and 'Gold Dust', both with heavily gold-spangled leaves and the latter also with fruits. For those who do not care for this type of virus-induced spotted variegation, the original plain green forms have lustrous, leathery, green leaves which, in female plants, are greatly enhanced by fruits resembling extra-large holly berries. Like the holly, aucubas have separate male and female plants, so at least one bush of each sex is necessary to get fruits. One male will pollinate several females. The purplish or bronzy green flowers are interesting but not conspicuous. 'Crassifolia' (male) has broad toothed leaves; 'Longifolia (female) has narrow, bright green leaves up to 5 in. (13 cm) long; and 'Salicifolia' (female) has even narrower, almost willow-like foliage as the name implies.

Berberis (barberry; see also p. 29) Approximately half the 450 species in this genus are evergreen and many are very garden-

---

Osmanthus delavayi, one of the finest flowering evergreens

43

worthy if one does not mind the spines. Readily available and with real quality is *Berberis verruculosa*. Densely clothed, it takes about 15 years to reach its maximum 6½ ft (2 m) in height. The small leaves are glossy green above and brightly blue-grey beneath – a marvellous contrast. In spring and then on and off until late summer, little bowl-shaped yellow flowers open, to be followed by blue-black berries. A confusing barberry, often seen in garden centres, is *B. × frikartii* 'Staefa', though it may be offered as *B. candidula* or with no name at all. It starts off like *B. candidula* (p. 53), but has longer leaves and, over a ten-year period, builds up into a dense rounded bush 5–6½ ft (1.5–2 m) tall. Temperate South America is the home of *B. linearifolia*, which produces in spring a profusion of bright orange flowers on arching stems, set against narrow, deep green leaves. Unfortunately, it is sparingly branched and usually becomes gaunt with old age. *Berberis × lologensis* is a natural hybrid between it and *B. darwinii* (p. 29), combining the best of both species.

Ceanothus (Californian lilac) Some of the best Californian lilacs are listed in the chapter on Large Shrubs (p. 30). In the medium-sized category, *Ceanothus* 'Burkwoodii' is outstanding, though it can exceed 6½ ft (2 m) if trained against a wall. It has oval, veiny, glossy, rich green leaves which are greyish downy beneath. Tiny, deep

Berberis verruculosa, from western China, is valuable for foliage, flowers and fruit

bright blue flowers open in clusters from just after midsummer to autumn. Although a sheltered site is required, it needs the protection of a wall only in very cold areas. This is also true for its probable parent, *C. dentatus*, a very distinctive species with tiny, elliptic, deep shiny green leaves having rolled-under margins and grey-felted undersides. Rounded clusters of bright blue flowers appear in early summer. Var. *floribundus* has broader leaves with less obviously rolled margins. It can be confused with *C.* × *veitchianus*, a taller shrub, with more-or-less wedge-shaped leaves (see p. 11), or with *C.* × *lobbianus*, also tall, with prominently three-veined, elliptic to oblong leaves ¾–1 in. (2–3 cm) long.

Choisya (Mexican orange blossom) Considering its Mexican homeland, *Choisya ternata* is remarkably hardy. Unusual among evergreen shrubs are its clover-like trifoliate leaves, which are a rich shiny green and pungently scented when bruised. It has a rounded habit and the white, fragrant, orange-blossom-like flowers are carried in terminal trusses, usually in abundance in spring, with a scattering into autumn. Both limy and acid soils are acceptable and some shade is tolerated.

Cistus (sun rose; see also p. 53) Whereas the majority of sun roses are small shrubs of unreliable hardiness, most of those that do

Choisya ternata will grow in shade, but flowers more profusely in sun

qualify as medium-sized are also the hardiest. Toughest of all is *Cistus laurifolius*, an erectly habited plant with dark, matt green, leathery, lance-shaped leaves. In summer, this somewhat sombre foliage is lit up with pure white 'roses' up to 3 in (7.5 cm) in diameter. Almost as hardy but shorter and with narrower, aromatic, less sombre leaves is the gum cistus, *C. ladanifer*. It also has larger finer flowers, each white petal having a basal blood-crimson blotch. *Cistus × cyprius*, the hybrid between the two species, in effect is a hardier, smaller-flowered *C. ladanifer*, but curiously has a more graceful habit than either parent. Tallest of all the sun roses is *C. populifolius*, often exceeding 6½ ft (2 m), with flowers rather like those of *C. laurifolius*. The leaves are most distinct – long-stalked, broadly oval and net-veined – certainly as near as any cistus is ever likely to get to those of a poplar.

Daphne (see also p. 54) *Daphne bholua* is the only evergreen daphne to be relied upon to grow 5 ft (1.5 m) or even 6½ ft (2 m) tall. Fairly sparingly branched and erect, its elliptic to lance-shaped leaves are 2–4 in. (5–10 cm) long and clustered towards the stem tips. From early or mid-winter to spring, clusters of tubular, four-petalled, very fragrant flowers appear. Generally they are purplish pink, but they can vary to almost white. The form 'Jacqueline Postill' has white flowers flushed rosy purple, while 'Sheopuri' is white flushed purple at the base and has a compact habit. Both are reasonably hardy and thrive in acid and alkaline soils.

Escallonia *Escallonia × rigida* is an umbrella name for the many floriferous hybrid cultivars so readily available. Most were raised at the Slieve Donard nursery in Northern Ireland and have Donard in their names. All are more-or-less evergreen, much depending upon the severity of the winter. Names to go for are 'Donard Beauty', with freely produced, rosy carmine blossom; 'Donard Gem', light pink; 'Donard Radiance', rich pink; 'Donard Seedling', white, flushed pale pink; and 'Apple Blossom', with flowers befitting its name. All well drained soils are acceptable.

Hebe (shrubby veronica; see also p. 54) Among the virtually hardy species in this popular genus of flowering evergreens, only *Hebe salicifolia* reaches and exceeds 6½ ft (2 m) in height. Rather more open in habit than most hebes, it has a rounded outline and toothed, palish green, willow-shaped leaves 2½–6 in. (6–15 cm) long. White or mauve-tinted flowers open in long tapered racemes during the summer. It is a parent of several of the hybrid cultivars, for example

'Miss E. Fittall', with 4–6 in. (10–15 cm) long racemes of mauve-blue flowers. The showiest of the taller species is *H. speciosa*, a robust plant having leathery, glossy leaves and spikes of red-purple flowers (see p. 13). Cultivars similar to and derived from it are 'Alicia Amherst' and 'Royal Purple', deep purple-blue; 'Gauntlettii', salmon-pink; 'La Seduisante', magenta-purple; and 'Simon Delaux', crimson. All are tender, requiring areas of minimal frost to thrive. However, they make excellent tub plants for the patio if kept under cover during frosty spells. They will grow in all soils.

Juniperus (juniper; see also p. 36) *Juniperus* × *media* 'Pfitzeriana' is an architectural plant which takes many years to exceed 6½ ft (2 m) in height. Always wider than high, it has layered horizontal branches with drooping tips. The sharp-pointed awl-shaped leaves are lightish green, but seem darker in certain lights. It makes a splendid specimen for the smaller lawn or at the end of a short vista. 'Pfitzeriana Aurea' has yellow young shoots and 'Pfitzeriana Glauca' is entirely grey to silver-green. For an extra-bright green, 'Mint Julep' is worth acquiring. Neutral to acid soil is best.

Leptospermum (tea tree, manuka) These somewhat heath-like shrubs, with their profusion of five-petalled flowers like tiny single roses, are mainly large in size but, as they are often cut back or killed in all but the mildest areas, 6½ ft (2 m) or a little more is a

Escallonia 'Apple Blossom' flowers throughout the summer

47

good average. The New Zealand *Leptospermum scoparium* is the best known, bearing ½ in. (12 mm) wide white flowers in summer; pink and red forms and doubles are known. From Australia comes *L. lanigerum*, a usually silky grey-hairy-leaved species with white flowers. It is definitely hardier than *L. scoparium* and, if not cut back by severe winter weather, can become a large shrub. Neutral to acid, well drained soil is required and a sunny sheltered site, ideally against a wall.

Lonicera The popular hedging plant, *Lonicera nitida* is seldom thought of as an ornamental species, but it can be a valuable one, at least in the short term. Allowed to grow naturally, its densely borne, tiny, glossy leaves produce dark billows against which larger brighter-leaved shrubs stand out most effectively. Several cultivars are known, 'Ernest Wilson' being the one commonly used for hedging; 'Yunnan' is more robust and has larger leaves; 'Fertilis' flowers and fruits profusely. The flowers are tiny, greenish and fragrant and the fruits are small translucent berries the colour of amethysts but rather hidden. Both the latter forms should be looked out for. 'Baggesen's Gold' is yellow-green in winter and yellow in summer.

Mahonia (see also p. 36) The Oregon grape, *Mahonia aquifolium*, is hardy and easy to please. The erect, sparingly branched stems sucker from the base and bear lustrous pinnate leaves composed of five to nine broadly oval leaflets. The bright yellow flowers erupt in conspicuous terminal clusters from late winter to late spring. The blue-black, bloomy fruits are like tiny grapes. Very similar, but superior in the gloss and general appearance of its wavy leaflets is *M.* 'Undulata'. Whereas *M. aquifolium* only rarely reaches 6½ ft (2 m), 'Undulata' regularly does and often exceeds it (see p. 6).

Myrtus (myrtle) In its western Asian homeland and in climates with little frost, the common myrtle, *Myrtus communis*, can form a large shrub or small tree. Against a sheltered wall in the British Isles, it often lasts for several years before getting killed. So, as a decorative, quick-growing, easy-to-propagate shrub, it is well worth considering in the short term. Aromatic, 1–2 in. (2.5–5 cm) long, dark glossy green, oval to lance-shaped leaves make a nice background for the clusters of fragrant white flowers, each with its prominent central brush of stamens. These open in late summer, usually on quite young plants, and may be followed by broadly oblong, purple berries. In the cultivar 'Variegata', the leaves are patterned white and, in 'Flore Pleno', the flowers are double. Var. *tarentina* is very distinctive, with its crowded half-size leaves.

Nandina (sacred or heavenly bamboo) There is only one species, *Nandina domestica*, in this Chinese genus, which is closely allied to *Berberis* yet has something of the elegance and appearance of a small bamboo. Much cultivated in Japan, where it is admired for the grace and beauty of its finely dissected leaves, it has never become well known in Britain. Branching mainly from the base, it is an erect plant 4–6½ ft (1.2–2 m) tall. The 10–18 in. (25–45 cm) long leaves start bronze, mature bright green and often take on purple or red tints in autumn and winter. Terminal clusters of small white flowers appear in summer and may be followed by red, yellow or white berries. Acid, moist soil and shade are necessary.

Olearia (daisy bush; see also p. 37) Hardiest of the New Zealand daisy bushes which can reach medium size in Great Britain is *Olearia × haastii*. Of rounded habit and with small oval leaves, matt green above and white-felted beneath, it becomes smothered every late summer with tiny, white daisy blossoms. After the first few seasons, growth is fairly slow and at least 15 years must pass before the 6½ ft (2 m) mark is reached. It is easily suited in a well drained soil and reasonably hardy unless the winter is really severe.

Osmanthus Superficially, several members of this genus might be mistaken for hollies, such is the nature of their tough spiny-margined leaves. However, the leaves of *Osmanthus* are in opposite pairs, while those of hollies are alternate. One of the best known is *O. heterophyllus*, formerly *O. aquifolium* and *O. ilicifolius*, both synonyms referring to its holly masquerade. Although not unlike common holly, it has a more rounded habit and flat, less glossy, deep green leaves. The small white flowers are not showy, but being borne in autumn and sweetly scented, they are most acceptable. The cultivar 'Myrtifolius' has spineless leaves and is rather more compact in habit, while 'Variegatus' has the leaves irregularly margined with creamy white. Contrasting dramatically with the latter is 'Purpureus', which has lustrous black-purple-tinted young growth, aging to deep purplish green.

Osmanthus decora (*Phillyrea decora*) is not at all like a holly, having almost willow-like, glossy leaves 2–5 in. (5–13 cm) long and small white flowers in spring. It is a handsome foliage shrub of rounded habit which deserves to be seen more often. This applies even more to *O. delavayi* (see p. 42). It has densely borne, deep green, oval leaves no more than 1 in. (2.5 cm) long, and regularly each spring produces a veritable foam of fragrant, white, tubular flowers – very different from the tiny stars of the other species. All are easily grown in ordinary soil, acid or alkaline, and tolerate partial shade. In severe winters young tips may get killed back.

Pieris One species comes into the medium-sized category – *Pieris japonica*. It is more compact than *P. formosa* (p. 38) and with smaller darker leaves. When young, the foliage is brownish red to coppery, though in the cultivar 'Bert Chandler' it is salmon-pink. The white flowers, often liberally produced, are borne in drooping panicles in spring. Several pink forms are available, for instance, 'Pink Delight', 'Blush' and 'Flamingo'. All these supersede 'Daisen' and 'Christmas Cheer'. 'Purity' is the best white. Moist acid soil is essential.

Rosmarinus (rosemary) Although common rosemary, *Rosmarinus officinalis*, can vary greatly in habit, the basic species is erect and bushy, eventually attaining 6½ ft (2 m) in height. As a dual-purpose herb and flowering shrub, it deserves a place in every garden. The attractive, spring-borne, tubular, two-lipped flowers are generally a pale violet-blue, but vary in shade. In cultivation, rosemary is represented by several named cultivars, best known being 'Miss Jessopp's Upright'. This has great vigour and slightly broader leaves than usual, with almost lavender-blue flowers. Of a clearer truer blue is 'Blue Spire', the leaves of which are narrower than the species. 'Tuscan Blue' has similar-coloured flowers and broad leaves of a distinctive lightish green. Best for flower colour is 'Benenden Blue', of almost gentian hue and with very narrow leaves. It is not so tall and has a semi-erect habit. A complete colour break is 'Majorca Pink', the flowers opening lilac-pink early in the year on erect broad-leaved bushes. Rosemaries grow in all well drained soils in sun, but can be damaged in severe winters. They make good tub plants.

Thuja (arbor vitae) Like its close allies *Chamaecyparis* (p. 21) and *Cupressus* (p. 22), *Thuja* has the stem entirely covered with overlapping scale-leaves when mature. In the seedling and young plant stage, however, the leaves are awl-shaped and spreading. In some cultivars, this juvenile foliage persists for the life of the plant. Thuyas are normally of tree size, but many bushy mutant cultivars

Thuja occidentalis 'Rheingold' is deservedly popular

are known, particularly of the American arbor vitae or so-called white cedar, *T. occidentalis*. Of these, 'Europe Gold' is a useful and eye-catching narrow pyramid of bright golden yellow scale-leaves, which take on orange hues in winter. It makes an interesting accent plant for a small lawn. The well known 'Rheingold' forms a broad, somewhat irregular cone of yellow to coppery orange juvenile leaves, the latter hue remaining through the winter. Older plants tend to develop scale-leaves. 'Smaragd' is rather like 'Europe Gold' in shape and size, but the foliage is emerald green the whole year. All moderately fertile soils are suitable.

Small Shrubs

A primary function of small shrubs is to fill in the front of a shrub bed or border, acting as ground cover and setting off the larger shrubs or small trees behind. They can also be attractive in their own right and deserve to be used more often in this way, for example, as a mosaic to fill a bed, border or bank where tall plants would be out of place. The less hardy small shrubs can be placed very effectively in a narrow border at the foot of a wall with, ideally, a background of climbers. Some of the more compact ones can be used as accent plants in a large rock garden.

Approximately 3 ft (1 m) is the upper limit of the shrubs described.

Berberis (barberry) Good evergreen barberries have been mentioned in the chapters on Large and Medium-sized Shrubs (p. 29 and p. 43) and equally fine ones occur among the smallest. One such is *Berberis candidula*, neatly bun-shaped, generally wider than high and taking many years to outgrow 3 ft (1 m) in height. The lustrous, dark green leaves are startlingly blue-white beneath, ½ –1 in. (1.5–3 cm) long, narrowly oval with rolled-under margins. Almost globose, bright yellow flowers of comparatively large size, up to ½ in. (1.5 cm) across, open in spring and are followed by purple-black berries. There are several small cultivars grouped under *B. × stenophylla* (p. 29), which favour the smaller parent, *B. empetrifolia*, in stature. Thus, 'Irwinii' reaches about 3 ft (1 m) in height and spread, while the foliage and flowers are nearer to *B. darwinii*. Deep yellow flowers are produced in profusion in late spring and early summer. *Berberis empetrifolia* is a highly distinctive species. In ten years or so, it can reach 15–24 in. (40–60 cm) in height and twice this in spread. The low arching stems are clad in very narrow, almost needle-like, dark green leaves with a greyish cast. The flowers are bright golden yellow wreathing all the stems abundantly in spring.

Cistus (sun rose; see also p. 45) In the small category are several delightful species and cultivars. *Cistus crispus* is one of the best of

Above: the grey-green leaves of *Cistus crispus* complement the flowers
Below: *Skimmia japonica*, with both flowers and fruits in April

these, having long, white-hairy shoots and grey-green narrowly oblong leaves with very wavy margins. The purplish red flowers are 1½ in. (4 cm) across and open in summer. *Cistus × skanbergii* is somewhat similar, but the leaves are greyer green and the plentifully produced smaller flowers a clear shade of pale pink. Well drained soil, acid or limy, and a sunny sheltered site are required.

Daphne (see also p. 46) For a really shaded site, *Daphne laureola* and *D. pontica* take some beating. Both have leathery, glossy, deep green leaves and clusters of yellow-green fragrant flowers in late winter and spring, those of *D. laureola* rather hidden under the leaves. Also shade-tolerant, but best in half-day sun is *D. odora*. Eventually reaching 2½–3 ft (75 cm–1 m) in height and more in width, it bears winter clusters of red-purple buds, which open to paler or almost white flowers with a piercingly sweet scent. There is a pure white-flowered form and also 'Aureo-marginata', the leaves of which have paler yellow margins. Smaller, neater and sun-loving are the almost identical *D. sericea* and *D. collina*. The oval, ¾–1½ in. (2–4 cm) long leaves are silky-hairy beneath and dark green above and make a good foil for the spring-borne red-purple flowers. Daphnes thrive in most fertile, well drained, but not dry soils.

Grevillea No member of this facinating Australian genus is really hardy, but the following two are well worth trying in warm sunny nooks, perhaps with some winter protection if the weather forecast is bad. *Grevillea rosmarinifolia* is the best known, an almost feathery shrub with dark grey-green, needle-like, sharply pointed leaves, silvery-hairy beneath. The summer-borne rosy red flowers are quite unlike those of most plants, consisting of a coloured tubular calyx which splits down one side and rolls back to disclose a long coloured style. *Grevillea sulphurea* is similar in height and habit, producing larger clusters of smaller, pale yellow flowers. Furthermore, it appears to be marginally hardier. Neutral to acid soil is recommended.

Hebe (shrubby veronica; see also p. 46) A wide variety of species and cultivars is now available of this deservedly popular but unreliably hardy genus. Among the species, *Hebe rakaiensis* is almost fully hardy. It forms a compact rounded bush of bright, almost yellow-green leaves and, when mature, produces an abundance of pure white flowers. It is often wrongly listed and sold as *H. subalpina*, a looser, darker green shrub, with longer leaves and a surprising vulnerability to winter frost. Equally as hardy as *H. rakaiensis* is *H. albicans*, with crowded leaves of bright grey-green and squat white flower spikes set off by purple anthers. Also with grey leaves, but much smaller and forming a bushlet up to about 16 in. (40 cm) is *H. topiaria* – just right for the larger rock garden. Of loose and spreading habit and with even smaller blue-grey leaves, *H. pimelioides* is a charmer which bears rich purple-blue flowers in summer.

Intriguingly different from the general run of hebes is the small group known as whipcord. These have tiny, overlapping, scale-like leaves, creating a very good imitation of a dwarf conifer. Most species are very small and best suited to the rock garden, but a few exceed 2 ft (60 cm) in time and one can reach 4 ft (1.2 m). This is the aptly named *Hebe cupressoides*, a rounded grey-green shrub just like a conifer until surrounded by a haze of minute lavender-tinted flowers. Very different is the 2 ft (60 cm) tall *H. ochracea*, a flattish-topped species which looks as though it had been lacquered in old gold. White flowers enhance the effect in summer.

Kalmia Although *Kalmia latifolia* (p. 36) is the finest member of its genus, the small *K. angustifolia* and *K. polifolia* are very attractive in their way. Both have an erect, rather open habit, *K. angustifolia* also suckering and forming small colonies. The flowers have the shape and charm of those of *K. latifolia*, but are smaller. In *K. polifolia* they are pale purplish rose, in *K. angustifolia* deep rose-red. Both need acid soil which does not dry out and at least half-day sun.

Hebe albicans is one of the more reliable hebes for hardiness

For the bushiest plants, *Pernettya mucronata* is best grown in a sunny position

Pernettya *Pernettya mucronata* is a perfect ground-covering small shrub. In the moist, but well drained, acid soil that suits it best, it suckers freely, sending up wiry stems densely clad with tiny deep green leaves, which are an ideal foil for the short spikes of little pure white bells in early summer. Later, comparatively large, globular berries ripen to shades of white and lilac-pink to red and purple. As individual seedlings or cultivars tend to be self-sterile or single-sexed, it is necessary to grow more than one plant for a good crop of berries. Recommended are 'Bell's Seedling', dark red fruits; 'Lilacina', lilac-pink; 'Mulberry Wine', magenta; and 'White Pearl'.

Prunus (laurel) Very distinct among the cherry laurels (p. 39) is the dwarf compact *Prunus laurocerasus* 'Otto Luyken'. It takes about ten years to reach 3–4 ft (1–1.2 m) in height and then steadily extends sideways, eventually to 6½ or even 10 ft (2–3 m) in width. The leaves are smaller and darker than other cherry laurel cultivars and the flowers more freely produced. (See p. 8.)

Sarcococca (sweet box) Although of modest appearance, the various kinds of sweet box are useful and pleasing. Very shade-tolerant – they will thrive in sunless north-facing borders – they provide a good low background or high ground cover between trees and tall shrubs. *Sarcococca hookeriana* is a suckering species with willow-shaped leaves. It can in time exceed 3 ft (1 m), but stands pruning and shearing after flowering. Sometimes confused are *S. ruscifolia* var. *chinensis* and *S. confusa*. Both have smallish, glossy deep green, oval to elliptic leaves, the first with red berries, the second with black ones. All sarcococcas have tiny fragrant flowers in winter. Although petal-less, they are easily visible as the fat white stamens have an almost luminous quality. Only in the smaller *S. hookeriana* var. *digyna* do the stamens take on pink tints. All soils are acceptable, ideally in sites sheltered from freezing winds.

Senecio (shrubby ragwort) Frequently seen in parks and gardens, especially near the sea, is *Senecio* 'Sunshine' (often listed as *S. greyi* or *S. laxifolius*). The leaves, white-felted beneath and cottony-hairy above when young, are oval and seldom more than 2½ in. (6 cm) in length. Around mid- to late summer, numerous panicles of bright yellow daisy flowers cover the bush. True *S. greyi* has leaves up to 4 in. (10 cm) long and much larger, looser panicles of flowers in early to mid-summer. Particularly attractive in leaf is *S. monroi*. Smaller than 'Sunshine', it has the leaf margins neatly and densely crimped, the felted white underside protruding as a frost-like rim. Well drained soil and sun are necessary for good results.

Skimmia Having good laurel-like leaves, winter-borne flowers and bright red berries, the skimmias are ideal plants for shady beds and borders and beneath trees. *Skimmia japonica* and its several variants are the hardiest and easily obtainable (see p. 52). The dense terminal clusters of fragrant white flowers are usually either male or female, so at least two plants are needed to get one freely fruiting. Partially hermaphrodite clones are known, but tend to fruit sparingly. Only in var. *reevesiana* (still often treated as a separate species, *S. reevesiana*) are both sexes present on the same plant to give a good crop of berries. This is dwarfer, under 2 ft (60 cm), and has red flower buds. It could be confused with the *S. japonica* cultivar, 'Rubella', although that grows up to about 4 ft (1.2 m) high and the red-budded flowers are entirely male. Good female forms are *S. × foremanii* and *S. japonica* 'Nymans'. Many other cultivars, some very dwarf, are now becoming available.

Viburnum (see also p. 40) Widely hummock-forming and eventually up to about 3 ft (1 m) in height, *Viburnum davidii* is one of the handsomest viburnums. The glossy leathery leaves are narrowly oval, up to 5 in. (13 cm) long and conspicuously veined. Small white flowers open in flattened heads and are followed by metallic blue berries. Ideally, at least two seed-raised plants should be planted side by side so that cross pollination can take place and a good crop of fruits result. Individual plants tend to fruit poorly or not at all.

Reasonably hardy evergreen climbers are few and far between. All are valuable in the garden, either on walls or pergolas, or scrambling through larger shrubs and trees.

Climbers attach themselves to a support in a variety of ways. Twining stems are the commonest method, but aerial roots (ivy) and twining or encircling leaf stalks (clematis) also occur.

Asteranthera The Latin *aster*, a star, and *anthera*, anther, allude to the joined anthers of *Asteranthera ovata*, which fancifully resemble a shooting star. Certainly, this self-clinging climber can be described as a star-turn, with its flame-red, 1 in. (3 cm) long flowers like those of the greenhouse *Columnea*. It looks best when growing up a tree trunk, as it usually does in the wild, where it creates a neat, rich green clothing of small oval leaves – the perfect background for its summer-borne flamboyant flowers. The only member of a genus from temperate South America, it needs little in the way of soil, thriving in peat or leafmould with a dash of bonemeal added each spring. Partial shade is best and a very sheltered site is required. Even then, severe winters can damage or decimate it.

Berberidopsis Like *Asteranthera*, this genus comes from South America and contains just the one species, *Berberidopsis corallina*. It is a twiner, with stems 6½–10 ft (2–3 m) in length, bearing lustrous, leathery, oblong to oval leaves 2–4 in. (5–10 cm) long. In summer and early autumn, showy pendent clusters of almost globular, ½ in. (1.5 cm) wide, crimson flowers appear. It is very much a climber of distinction, though one could wish that it were hardier. However, on a sheltered, partly shaded wall in acid peaty soil, it usually survives all but severe winters.

Clematis A truly imposing climber is *Clematis armandii* from China. Rapidly climbing to 20 ft (6 m) or more, it has trifoliate leaves composed of narrowly oval leaflets 3–6 in. (8–15 cm) in length. These are bronzy when young, maturing to deep lustrous green. In spring, clusters of white or cream flowers, about 2–2½ in. (5–6 cm)

Euonymus fortunei var. *radicans* clothes a wall most attractively wide, expand from the leaf axils, nicely set off by the dark foliage. The cultivar 'Snowdrift' has pure white flowers, while 'Apple Blossom' is pink-flushed. Quite different is *C. cirrhosa*, a slender climber up to 10 ft (3 m), with elegant ferny leaves and nodding bell-shaped flowers during winter and spring. Var. *balearica* is rather more decorative, the flowers being flushed and spotted red-purple. Both species will grow in most soils, but must have a sheltered aspect.

Euonymus *Euonymus fortunei* var. *radicans* clings to its support by aerial roots and forms a neat close cover to a wall (see p. 58). It also makes an effective ground cover. The foliage is carried in pairs, each oval, smooth, rich green leaf ½–1 in. (1.5–3 cm) long. The variegated sorts are popular, notably 'Variegatus', with the leaves broadly white-bordered. Like ivy, mature plants produce non-climbing branches, which have insignificant flowers and pinkish fruits with orange seeds. Most soils and sites are suitable.

Holboellia The twining *Holboellia coriacea* from China has trifoliate leaves not unlike those of *Clematis armandii*. In bloom, however, it is totally different. The flowers are unisexual, with males and females on the same plant. They are bell-shaped, borne in nodding clusters, the males small and white, the females larger and greenish white flushed purple, expanding in spring. Fleshy purple fruits up to 2 in. (5 cm) long may develop. A sheltered site, moist humus-rich soil and at least half-day sun are needed.

Lapageria (Chilean bellflower) *Lapageria rosea*, the Chilean bell-flower, or copihue as it is known in its native country, is the national flower of Chile and it would be difficult indeed to select anything finer as the emblem of a country. Wiry twining stems, which can grow 10–16 ft (3–5 m) in length, bear oval, almost glossy, leathery, deep green leaves up to 4 in. (10 cm) long. During summer and autumn, a succession of slenderly bell-shaped, pendent flowers appears. These are about 3 in. (8 cm) long, sometimes more, composed of six waxy, fleshy-textured tepals of lustrous crimson, which are lighter-flecked within. The form 'Albiflora' has rose-tinted white flowers, and 'Nash Court' soft rich pink ones (see p. 8). Humus-rich soil and a sheltered site are necessary.

Mitraria A member of the tropical gesneriad family and the only known species of *Mitraria*, *M. coccinea* is no more than a weak scrambler, but is splendid when encouraged to push its way through a companion shrub. If left to itself, it tends to make a low spreading shrub. The small, glossy, oval leaves are a lovely foil for the scarlet, pendent, bottle-shaped flowers, which appear in summer and autumn. The Chilean vernacular name, botellita, is most apt. Humus-rich acid soil and a sheltered, partially shaded position are essential requirements.

Pileostegia A member of the same family as *Hydrangea*, but looking more like a viburnum in leaf and flower, *Pileostegia viburnoides* is another root climber like ivy. Suitable for sunny and shady walls alike, this attractive species is rather slow-growing when young. Eventually, however, it can reach 16 ft (5 m) or more in height and then looks very effective on a tall tree trunk. The strongly veined, leathery leaves are more or less oval and from 2½–6 in. (6–15 cm) long. In early autumn, terminal panicles of tiny milky white flowers with long stamens are a welcome sight. Reasonably hardy, it thrives in a humus-rich soil which does not dry out, and tolerates some lime.

Stauntonia Closely related to *Holboellia*, the Japanese *Stauntonia hexaphylla* is well worth trying on a sheltered wall or up a tree. Capable of twining to 33 ft (10 m) in height, it has fingered leaves formed of three to seven dark green, oval leaflets, each 2½–5 in. (7–13 cm) long. The fragrant, white, purple-tinted flowers are unisexual, the males and females in separate racemes on the same plant in spring. Warm springs and summers may see 2 in. (5 cm) long, egg-shaped, purplish fruits developing, which are edible but insipid. Humus-rich neutral to acid soil is best.

Trachelospermum Only two members of this genus are reasonably hardy. Both have the appeal of a jasmine, but the leaves are small, simple, oval and leathery textured. Both also seem to combine twining with aerial roots as a means of support. Hardiest is *Trachelospermum asiaticum* (including *T. majus* and *T. japonicum*), with ¾ in. (2 cm) wide flowers, which open white and become yellow in late summer. *Trachelospermum jasminoides* is the handsomer, having larger leaves and flowers which stay white. The cultivar 'Variegatum' produces leaves which are irregularly cream-bordered and blotched. 'Wilsonii' has the leaf veins picked out in creamy green and the stems appear to climb mainly by aerial roots. Most soils are acceptable and a sheltered, fairly sunny site is needed for reliable flowering.

A Selection of Evergreens for Particular Purposes

Hedges
Berberis darwinii
B. × stenophylla
Cotoneaster lacteus
Escallonia
Euonymus japonicus
Ilex aquifolium
Laurus nobilis
Lonicera nitida
Osmanthus × burkwoodii
Olearia
Phillyrea
Photinia
Pittosporum tenuifolium
Prunus laurocerasus
P. lusitanica
Viburnum tinus

Windbreaks
Abies delavayi
Chamaecyparis lawsoniana
Drimys winteri
Hoheria sexstylosa
Ilex × altaclerensis
I. aquifolium
Laurus nobilis
Magnolia grandiflora
Pittosporum tenuifolium
Prunus laurocerasus
Quercus ilex
Thuja occidentalis

Ground cover
Euonymus fortunei var. radicans
Hebe albicans
H. rakaiensis
Juniperus × media 'Pfitzeriana'
Mahonia aquifolium
Pernettya mucronata
Prunus laurocerasus 'Otto Luyken'
Sarcococca
Senecio 'Sunshine'
Viburnum davidii

Coastal sites
Arbutus
Cistus
Choisya ternata
Elaeagnus
Escallonia
Eucalyptus
Euonymus fortunei
E. japonicus
Fatsia japonica
Garrya elliptica
Hebe
Ilex aquifolium
Juniperus
Laurus nobilis
Lonicera nitida
Olearia
Phillyrea
Pittosporum
Quercus ilex
Rosmarinus officinalis
Senecio 'Sunshine'
Viburnum tinus

Shade
Asteranthera ovata
Aucuba japonica
Cephalotaxus harringtonia
Choisya ternata
Daphne laureola
Elaeagnus
Euonymus fortunei
Fatsia japonica
Ilex aquifolium
Juniperus × media 'Pfitzeriana'
Lapageria rosea
Mahonia aquifolium
Mitraria coccinea
Nandina domestica
Pileostegia viburnoides
Prunus laurocerasus
P. lusitanica
Sarcococca

Skimmia japonica
Viburnum davidii
V. 'Pragense'
V. rhytidophyllum

Acid soil essential
Arbutus menziesii
Berberidopsis corallina
Crinodendron hookerianum
Desfontainia spinosa
Embothrium coccineum
Eucryphia
Ilex pedunculosa
Kalmia
Mitraria coccinea
Nandina domestica
Pernettya mucronata
Pieris

Suitable for limy soils
Berberis (except B. empetrifolia)
Ceanothus
Cistus
Cotoneaster
Euonymus fortunei
E. japonicus
Hebe
Ilex aquifolium
Juniperus
Lonicera nitida
Mahonia aquifolium
Olearia
Phillyrea
Rosmarinus officinalis
Sarcococca
Senecio
Thuja occidentalis
Viburnum

Wall shrubs
Abelia
Ceanothus
Choisya ternata
Cistus
Daphne
Drimys winteri
Escallonia
Feijoa sellowiana
Fremontodendron
Garrya elliptica
Hebe

Hoheria
Itea ilicifolia
Laurus nobilis
Leptospermum
Magnolia grandiflora
Mahonia
Myrtus communis
Olearia
Pittosporum
Pyracantha
Rosmarinus officinalis
Sarcococca
Viburnum tinus

Town gardens
Abelia
Arbutus
Azara microphylla
Berberis (small species)
Ceanothus
Cordyline
Choisya ternata
Cistus
Crinodendron hookerianum
Daphne
Drimys winteri
Elaeagnus
Embothrium coccineum
Escallonia
Eucalyptus
Eucryphia
Fatsia japonica
Fremontodendron
Garrya elliptica
Hebe
Itea ilicifolia
Kalmia
Laurus nobilis
Mahonia
Nandina domestica
Pernettya mucronata
Pieris
Pyracantha
Rosmarinus officinalis
Sarcococca
Senecio
Skimmia
Viburnum davidii

Variegated foliage
Cultivars of:
Abelia × grandiflora

Aucuba japonica
Azara microphylla
Daphne odora
Elaeagnus pungens
Euonymus fortunei
E. japonicus
Hoheria populnea
Ilex × altaclerensis
I. aquifolium
Myrtus communis
Pieris japonica
Pittosporum tenuifolium
Prunus lusitanica
Viburnum tinus
Trachelospermum jasminoides

Showy flowers
Abelia
Asteranthera ovata
Berberidopsis corallina
Berberis darwinii
B. empetrifolia
B. linearifolia
B. × stenophylla
B. valdiviana
Ceanothus
Cistus
Choisya ternata
Clematis armandii
C. cirrhosa var. balearica
Crinodendron hookerianum
Daphne bholua
D. odora
D. sericea
Desfontainia spinosa
Embothrium coccineum
Escallonia
Eucryphia
Fremontodendron
Garrya elliptica
Hebe
Hoheria
Kalmia
Lapageria rosea
Leptospermum
Magnolia grandiflora
Mahonia japonica
M. lomariifolia
Mitraria coccinea
Myrtus communis

Olearia
Osmanthus delavayi
Pieris japonica
Prunus laurocerasus
P. lusitanica
Skimmia japonica

Fragrant flowers
Abelia × grandiflora
Acacia dealbata
Azara microphylla
Choisya ternata
Clematis armandii
C. cirrhosa var. balearica
Daphne bholua
D. laureola
D. odora
Drimys winteri
Elaeagnus
Itea ilicifolia
Magnolia grandiflora
Mahonia japonica
M. × media
Myrtus communis
Olearia
Osmanthus
Pittosporum tenuifolium
Sarcococca
Skimmia japonica
Stauntonia hexaphylla
Trachelospermum jasminoides

Conspicuous fruits
Abies delavayi
A. koreana
Arbutus
Aucuba japonica
Berberis (most)
Cephalotaxus harringtonia
Cotoneaster
Euonymus japonicus
Ilex (most)
Mahonia aquifolium
Pernettya mucronata
Prunus laurocerasus
P. lusitanica
Pyracantha
Skimmia japonica
Viburnum davidii
V. rhytidophyllum